How to Write an eBook Bestseller

Easy Steps to Write a Non-Fictional Bestseller

Daniel Kern

Bibliografische Information der Deutschen Nationalbibliothek:

Die Deutsche Nationalbibliothek verzeichnet diese Publikation in der Deutschen Nationalbibliografie; detaillierte bibliografische Daten sind im Internet über http://dnb.dnb.de abrufbar.

© 2021, Daniel Kern, 2nd Edition

Title Picture: Andrew E. Larsen @Flickr under CC License

Herstellung und Verlag: BoD –
Books on Demand, Norderstedt

ISBN: 978-3-7534-2013-4

Introduction

By using this book, you accept this disclaimer in full.

No advice

The book contains information. The information is not advice and should not be treated as such.

No representations or warranties

To the maximum extent permitted by applicable law and subject to section below, we exclude all representations, warranties, undertakings and guarantees relating to the book.

Without prejudice to the generality of the foregoing paragraph, we do not represent, warrant, undertake or guarantee:

- that the information in the book is correct, accurate, complete or non-misleading.

- that the use of the guidance in the book will lead to any particular outcome or result.

Limitations and exclusions of liability

The limitations and exclusions of liability set out in this section and elsewhere in this disclaimer: are subject to section 6 below; and govern all liabilities arising under the disclaimer or in relation to the book, including liabilities arising in contract, in tort (including negligence) and for breach of statutory duty.

We will not be liable to you in respect of any losses arising out of any event or events beyond our reasonable control.

We will not be liable to you in respect of any business losses, including without limitation loss of or damage to profits, income, revenue, use, production, anticipated savings, business, contracts, commercial opportunities or goodwill.

We will not be liable to you in respect of any loss or corruption of any data, database or software.

We will not be liable to you in respect of any special, indirect or consequential loss or damage.

Exceptions

Nothing in this disclaimer shall: limit or exclude our liability for death or personal injury resulting from negligence; limit or exclude our liability for fraud or fraudulent misrepresentation; limit any of our liabilities in any way that is not permitted under applicable law; or exclude any of our liabilities that may not be excluded under applicable law.

Severability

If a section of this disclaimer is determined by any court or other competent authority to be unlawful and/or unenforceable, the other sections of this disclaimer continue in effect.

If any unlawful and/or unenforceable section would be lawful or enforceable if part of it were deleted, that part will be deemed to be deleted, and the rest of the section will continue in effect.

Law and jurisdiction

This disclaimer will be governed by and construed in accordance with Swiss law, and any disputes relating to this disclaimer will be subject to the exclusive jurisdiction of the courts of Switzerland.

Inhaltsverzeichnis

Inhaltsverzeichnis	**9**
EBOOKS	**11**
WRITING AN EBOOK BESTSELLER	13
7 EASY STAPS TO WRITE A NON-FICTIONAL BESTSELLER	19
1. SUBJECT	*19*
2. RESEARCH	*20*
3. TITLE	*24*
4. AUDIENCE	*27*
5. STRUCTURE	*31*
1. The Opening Statements or Product/Subject:	33
2. Your opinion about the Subject/s or Product/s:	34
3. Pictures:	34
4. Readable Content:	35
5. Helpfulness:	35
6. Legal Stuff:	36
7. Affiliate Links:	37
8. Thank You:	37
For Pleasure -	38

6. PROMOTION	*39*
1. Testimonials might do the Trick	40
2. Include an 'About the Author' section	40
3. Increase Readability	41
4. Search Engines and Keywords	41
7. THE SELLING PRICE	*42*

HOW TO TURN YOUR EBOOK INTO A BESTSELLER **46**

EBOOKS

Ebooks are electronic gadgets which are quite similar to the iPods in that they have been especially designed for making lives easier and more convenient. The concept of online ebooks is so useful that it provides the users with all the necessary information that they are looking for. In common words, ebooks can well be described as an electronic method of reading books.

You can buy ebooks over the Internet from eBook publishers. Some of the ebooks can be downloaded either at a reduced cost or for free. Although there will not be much of a difference in the prices for many of the bestseller ebooks, it may be quite similar to the hardcover books, and at times higher than that as well.

In addition, it has so many advantages such as there is no paper, they are a quick way to purchase a book, the book downloads immediately to your computer or your eBook reader and you can begin to enjoy what you purchased over the Internet right away.

Moreover, ebooks can take up to 6,800 page turns in an eBook reader before powering down. You can get enough time to read "War and Peace" four times over. Ebooks have many features compared to traditional paper books.

WRITING AN EBOOK BESTSELLER

Writing and selling eBooks are one way of earning extra income at home, where you are not required to come up with financial capitals. This is different to any other type of online venture which focus on providing extra income for you. The key to a successful EBook is to learn how to create a bestselling EBook based on the experiences of other people who are already successful in this particular online niche.

Like any book, an interesting cover will attract the eye of people. This includes the title of the book being very important. But it isn't the cover that keeps them. Most people will sit and read a few paragraphs to see if it is either exciting, informative or interesting enough for them to buy the book. If a reader is reading the book and begins to skip lines (You know what I mean) like they are on line two of a paragraph and skip to the next paragraph before finishing the first paragraph, chances are that they don't like what they are reading. They will also, sometimes scan through the indexed content or chapters to see if they find something that they can relate to or are interested in.

Well eBook writing is the same with the exception that eBook covers are not what usually catches the readers attention it is the Title of the eBook. Yes, the cover or graphic you have to display your eBook may attract the reader, but not in most cases.

You are probably wondering how learning to write an eBook could possibly make you any significant amount of money. The fact is that eBooks have recently experienced a huge boom in sales over the past few years. People are interested in eBooks because they are able to get the information any regular book has to offer, but they can usually get extras as well (and the downloads are instant). The eBook typically comes in a PDF file which means the person can read it on their computer or print it off. If they don't want to take up extra shelf space in their house, they don't have to. This makes an eBook a viable choice for people who don't have much room to spare. Being cheaper and easier to use, it is no wonder eBooks have become so popular. If you want to learn how to write an eBook that could become a bestseller, read the information below.

When learning how to write an eBook that will sell enough copies to make you real money, you have to first consider the topic. Many people write topical eBooks. These take advantage of current situations with the economy or news that are popular searches. Since most people purchase eBooks to learn how to make money, financial eBooks are very popular. When the housing market is down, many people are searching for eBooks which will teach them how to buy and sell houses for a profit. If you are a skilled writer, you may be able to choose your own topic.

However, if you want to learn how to write an eBook about a specific topic which you are very knowledgeable, you may just be interested in learning proper formats for eBooks. If you already have the knowledge you need on the topic, writing in a manner which will best convey your information is important. The good news is that an eBook does not have a set format for success. eBooks should always be written very simply, but you do not have to adhere to any specific format in order to make a successful eBook.

Marketing an eBook is half the battle. Learning how to write an eBook will do you little good if no one sees it. If you are writing on a popular topic, you may find it hard to compete with these other, already established eBooks in your niche of choice. If you are serious about selling your eBook, there are some programs which will allow you to develop a website which has everything you need in order to get started. It will rank high in search engine results and give you the tools to sell and deliver your eBook instantly. While these programs are not always necessary, they are very helpful to someone who has never written or sold an eBook before.

Learning how to write an eBook is a great way to make extra money without having to commute to a job. It can be done in your spare time and at you leisure. Once you have some experience writing eBooks, you will find that additional eBooks become easier and easier to write; and if you write useful eBooks which people find helpful, you will have a base for further sales.

eBooks are not just to produce a new product for launch like an online program to help people make money online with certain techniques, it can be a FREE eBook giveaway to promote a niche or a product you have a campaign about.

7 EASY STAPS TO WRITE A NON-FICTIONAL BESTSELLER

In the steps below I have outlined how to go about writing a best seller:

1. SUBJECT

Now this is a place where most people get stuck. And of course if your not the writing type and your doing this for a niche (Product your promoting or affiliate marketing) then it can be a task looked upon as very difficult. But remember, if your writing an eBook (Electronic Book) then this means that you have access to a computer and Internet. So in turn, it becomes a little easier. You have the world right at your finger tips to do all the research you need. For me this is the most difficult and boring part...lol. writing about it is easy. A few suggestions: First, what are the reasons for this eBook: Profits, Enjoyment, Teaching. Whatever it may be figure this out first. If this doesn't help make a list of things you enjoy e.g. Hobbies, Sports, Trades, etc. One other thing you can do is make a list of things you know well and can do for hours or talk about for hours because basically, a eBook is just your words in a computer generated book. So the more you know, the more you like the subject, or the more you believe in the product or subject the better the book will turn out and the easier it is to produce and sell.

2. RESEARCH

This part takes the longest and can be very time consuming, but with proper keyword searches it can go pretty fast. Then there's the matter of compiling the information into a effective or attractive format to your readers. Now if your an expert on the subject, all the better. This will make the task of research much easier.

For Profit - If your writing for profit, One thing I do recommend when doing your research, if at all possible (unless it's a completely new subject or type of product), get some content in your eBook that talks about how good the product/s or subject/s your talking about is. Some testimonials from other authors, teachers, etc. that will justify your words of wisdom or your products. Now if your doing this eBook for a certain niche (Affiliate Product/s) and don't know to much about the product/s, find everything you can to help you gain knowledge of the product/s (Affiliate Campaigns). This will help you for one, know if the product/s is any good, two, familiarize you with the product/s and three, give you writing material to promote the product/s. Research for a new product like an eBook for teaching people how to do something and it's for profit, your research will be different. You must research your competitors sites, one, to help you know your competition and who they are and their techniques (If you can find the information or may already have purchased it), two, to be able to explain with conviction how your product or eBook is better (In Detail if possible, comparisons) and three, build your Authority status by referring to several topics about your product in detail thus showing your readers and potential consumers you know what your talking about.

For Exposure - This is the FREE eBook I mentioned earlier. This can either be a eBook to get people to buy your product/s (Promoted Affiliate Product/s) or interest them in a New product/s launch coming soon. It is also generally used on an opt-in page to create a email mailing list for further advertisements. Follow the steps above for this eBook as well.

For Pleasure - This is easy. You don't expect to make money in most cases and your basically writing about stuff you like whether it is teaching or a activity. Again, do some research on the subject as to add more content for your readers to have fun reading about what you like e.g. Hiking: Talk about all the places you have hiked and do some research on places you would like to go and hike so the reader will be interested in coming back to read more upon your next entry. Talk about some funny or embarrassing moments for laughs and stuff like this.

3. TITLE

A good title will sell your ebook. It is really as simple as that. A good title will attract attention and people will want to at least look into what you have on offer. Conversely, a poor title will be hidden amongst the other similar ebooks and will almost certainly go unnoticed. With no-one even looking at it there is little chance of any successful sales.

This is the most important part of the eBook. After you have chosen your subject and have done all your research you must then come up with a catchy or exciting title. A dull or boring title will have people just pass right by your eBook without a second glance. It is the second glance that draws them in. They see the title and then, BAMM, they have to look again. And now they want to know more about it. So really put a lot of effort into this part, because you only get one shot with each person on first glance. Of course if you spam the airwaves about your eBook and they see lots of articles about it they may come back, but the best shot you have is the first one, remember, First Impressions.

So, what makes a good title? Well the answer is something attention grabbing that makes a promise. A title such as "A Better Golf Swing" might describe what it does, but there are so many golf swing fixes that the title would just be hidden amongst the pile of many other titles. What makes your particular eBook unique? Why should someone buy your eBook when they have possibly already bought 10 different ebooks promising "A Better Golf Swing"?

That is the key to your title for your ebook. Find your unique selling point and describe it in a few words. Some people get overly concerned with trying to fit in as many keywords as they can in the title in the hope of search engine optimising at this point, but that is missing the aim of the task. The title that you choose for your eBook is meant to appeal to people, not search engines. You want to sell it to people who have seen the name on a list of titles, the search engine optimisation comes only when the book is completed.

And this isn't just true for the people who are buying the book. You will make the selling of your book a lot easier by using affiliate schemes such as ClickBank. So your title needs to also attract the attention of affiliates so that they see it as something different that they can sell on their websites. A spammy title might never be picked up, whereas a good interesting title might grab the interest of loads of affiliates and generate lots of sales very quickly.

Of course, it is not all about just thinking up a title and putting that at the top of your page. If you are going to be selling through ClickBank and other schemes then you should check before you start that the name you have chosen is not already the title of an existing publication. If you dreamt up a perfect title and did not check that no one else is using it and then loaded it to ClickBank you could be left in the awkward position of having copied someone else's title. If this title was popular not only would you look daft, but you could be accused of trying to benefit from their reputation.

4. AUDIENCE

Now depending on the subject or product your writing about this will make a difference in your writing. If you go to a comedy club, you are expecting good comedians, right. So you are going their for entertainment and hopefully to get a good laugh. Same when writing your eBook, you must calculate who your targeted audience will be, if any e.g. youth, elders, sports, etc.

In some cases you can leave it as targeted to the general public but not recommend. A more targeted audience will generate more income for you if this is what your eBook is about.

Whom Do You Wish to Serve?

When you write an ebook, you are serving the needs of a target market, in other words the people in your chosen niche. So ask yourself the question, "Whom do you wish to serve?" Many people overlook this very important aspect of the eBook writing activity. When you know who you are writing the eBook for, you're headed off in a purposeful direction.

For example, suppose you desire to write an eBook for employees experiencing stress. An eBook containing stress reduction ideas for one company may be completely inappropriate for another company. One company may encourage the submission of an eBook for the benefit of employees, while others would minimize this idea as useless for them.

Do Your Research

if you read an eBook for a business, go to their website and see what their mission needs are. That will be the same of the company. Make sure you write your eBook within the same of the company mission. If you do it successfully, the company may buy the eBook and hire you to write more ebooks. Good things come in electronic packages.

Write Your eBook to the Mindset of Your Target Audience

Pretend for a moment that you are the recipient of your ebook. What would be the reason for you to purchase this particular ebook? What would you be thinking? What would you be feeling? What are some of your most pressing problems or desires you think about often that could be solved by reading this specific ebook's information?

The mindset of the target audience can sometimes be practical, impractical, or emotional. The more you learn about your market, the more you're going to figure out how to promote your product. Your target audience's mindset is one of a thinking style. Would you can understand what that mindset is, and market to them, you increase your chances of selling many ebooks.

Your eBook Contains the Magic Answer

Get a piece of paper and pencil or open up a word processing document. Collect or write out complaints that your target audience is expressing. When you hear the complaint, that is a cry for a solution. You can write a solution, in a specific eBook that your audience will love.

So make sure you listen to all the details of the complaint. There will be many of them. The complaint can be the mindset. Listen to the complaint like it is impersonal feedback and pick and choose the information that you find will be the most helpful to your audience.

5. STRUCTURE

Now you can begin to build your structure of your book. You have the research, title and audience focus. Now it's time to fill the body of the eBook. The way you structure your book will either captivate your readers or put them to sleep and we don't want them sleeping half way through your ebook. Again there are a few different ways to structure your eBook.

For Profit or Exposure - Promoting a product/s, it is necessary to keep them excited all the way through. Also, make sure to explain everything your talking about in simple,easy to understand words. Unless this is a High Tech eBook, complicated and big words are not necessary, the simpler the better (But not childish).

1. The Opening Statements or Product/Subject:

Be specific and very welcoming to your audience. Make them feel like you appreciated them and get them excited real quick. Give some details about yourself and some explanation about the Product/Subject before the pitch.

2. Your opinion about the Subject/s or Product/s:

This is where you give your expertise on what it is that you are writing about and testimonials to reinforce that structure. This is also where you can do some lite pitching about the Product/s or subject/s. Make sure you keep the excitement levels high here to draw them to the bottom of the page if they don't hop on in the first lite pitch you spring on them.

3. Pictures:

It is also good to use some good visuals within your eBook to help your readers relate to your Product/s or Subject/s a little better. You can include pictures of your techniques, profits, software features and much more. I do recommend this as it adds to the professionalism of the eBook. A nice looking header at the top of your first page would be great as well.

4. Readable Content:

Make sure that you use a nice font like Verdana or Tahoma about 10 to 12 point for easy reading. It is important that the text is easy to read. This is for Profit, Exposure or Pleasure writing.

5. Helpfulness:

Make sure that your writings give the readers something that is helpful to them. If you help people you gain respect. Helpful tips are a great thing, it builds rapport with your readers. It also is good (If applicable) to make sure that if your book is about helping people that you recognize what their problems could be (According to the Topic) and you and address them in full detail. It will help you in the future if you ever recommend anything else or launch your own product someday, you will have a loyal audience to pitch to.

6. Legal Stuff:

Make sure that you let people know that you make no guarantees that the product creates success, you know the legal stuff. Everyone does things different, even if you let them know that following the program or product step by step will make them money, there are always situations that could and will arise that you have no control over and making 100% guarantees is a bit dangerous.

7. Affiliate Links:

If your doing this to sell Affiliate products, make sure you leave room to put your ads within your body content. Example. Your product is strategies and techniques for making money online. Leave a spot either for a text link, opt-in area that leads to the sale page or picture link for your products. You can also put other products to sell within the text body as well if you have several products. Make sure they are related in some way to each other.

8. Thank You:

Finish up with a thank you area expressing your thanks for them taking their time to download your eBook, purchase your eBook or your product/s. This is also a good place to show a few more of the products you have if any that you may not have shown through the other parts of the eBook.

For Pleasure -

1. You can follow the same structure, just leave out all the affiliate marketing talk. 2. Basically and intro of yourself, The body of your story and a ending with a Thank You to your readers. It really depends on what your doing with your eBook.

6. PROMOTION

Go out and promote your eBook where you can, build a Pitch Page/Landing Page and use the same techniques you used in your eBook to keep the excitement going all through the page with testimonials, visuals, profits you made (If applicable) and an opt-in area if this is for a FREE eBook. Make some article write-ups, a Blog or Website or articles for further information about yourself, your eBook and other product/s you may be promoting. And now you can call yourself a genuine Author.

Promotion is the key to selling any product or service. If you don't promote it then you are staring at a barrel full of losses. Therefore it's important that you have ideas for the promotion of ebooks in your armory so that you are never short of good sales figures. Here are 4 tips that will help you in promoting your ebooks.

1. Testimonials might do the Trick

You must try and include testimonials for the eBook that you are trying to sell. Make sure that you have not fudged the testimonials. They must be authentic and genuine and commensurate with the quality of the eBook in question.

2. Include an 'About the Author' section

When you buy a book, you usually buy one from a reputed author. The same is the case with the ebooks. Selling ebooks will get a whole lot easier if you put in a good word or two about the author and the books he/she has written previously.

3. Increase Readability

It's an eBook and hence the type of fonts and the font size is within your purview. The books should be readable. If you look at ebooks sales figures, you will find that easy to read ebooks are sold more than those that aren't so easy to read.

4. Search Engines and Keywords

Use search engines and keywords for selling ebooks. Create a marketing page that will talk about the ebooks that you are trying to sell. Finally don't follow the beaten bath with respect to promotion. Devise new strategies for selling ebooks.

7. THE SELLING PRICE

If this is your first whirl in the world of eBook sales you will really want to price your product competitively. After you've tasted a little success and you have a following, you can up your price. People are always looking for deals and eBooks are no exception.

There are some people that will sell a 100 page eBook for less than a dollar. This strategy works to drastically increase your eBook sales and reviews on sites like Amazon, which will allow you to climb the bestselling book ladder and increasing the value of your product by word of mouth marketing.

I need to add more information on this point. While there are several schools of thought about charging less to get your e-book out there and charging more so people believe they are getting high powered information that costs more. Not every method is suitable for every product. You should be doing your niche research to see where the gaps are in your targeted e-book audience and charging accordingly.

Now that the basic concepts of adding value to your eBook have been addressed, I would like to cover some more advanced ideas on ensuring that you have created a professional and saleable eBook and how you can spin that content into other profitable avenues.

It really doesn't matter if you're writing an eBook to make money or offer a broader service or product to your audience. It is the final product that must be attractive, valuable and profitable for you.

So by now you've written a 100 page eBook with unique, interesting quality content. You can use what you've written and turn it into a series of quality videos.

Now you have not only an awesome 100 page eBook but a video series to accompany it. You can continue by making that e-book into an audio book. And now you have:

- A 100 page eBook, 20 videos and 15 audios.

You can now increase your selling price because you are offering more. You could also make "cliff notes" with a short 1 or 2 page summary of each e-book chapter, then take this and create a members only blog where you can post this info for your members to ask questions on. After that you can find some people that you respect and admire in your niche and interview them for additional content. And after you finish that there are plenty of left over information that you can use to make another series about what you have learned along the way. Now you have:

- 100 page eBook, 20 videos 15 audios 13 cliff notes 10 master class interviews and 30 pages of content about tips and tricks learned along the way.

The value of your original eBook has substantially increased. Now you can create an upsell, by offering-mail coaching for $$$ a month, weekly coaching calls for $$$ a month also and so on and so forth.

After you complete that you can find out what are the most common problems your audience is facing and create a teleseminar to address them. You could set up a live event for your customers, and find someone to film it and make additional products; DVD's or stream the video from the event.

HOW TO TURN YOUR EBOOK INTO A BESTSELLER

Writing a bestseller is the Holy Grail of eBook and book writing. It is the one title that surpasses any other. It doesn't matter why you are writing eBooks. If you are writing eBooks for the purposes of making money it almost guarantees that your next books will make money. If you are writing eBooks for the purposes of branding it almost single-handedly turns you into the expert in your field.

Why?

It's another case of the print market affecting perceptions in the eBook market. Because it is so hard for a writer to produce a bestseller in the traditional market, people automatically presume that an eBook bestseller must be an expert too.

So how can you create a bestseller in the eBook market?

There are five techniques that need to combine in order to create a bestselling eBook. Of course, there is no guarantee even then. And sometimes a bestseller will arise for no discernable reason.

First off, it has become much easier to have a bestseller now that Amazon and Barnes and Noble are selling eBooks and print-on-demand books. You need to take advantage of the market strength of those two booksellers. Besides, each of them publishes their own bestsellers list giving you two chances to be on the bestsellers list.

Second you need to treat this as if it were a product launch. Build up demand. Take a week or two and begin to market heavily.

Very heavily. Then launch. If you were successful in your marketing, the pent up demand will push your eBook into the bestsellers list. At least for a short time.

Third you need to market heavily to your own customer list. They already know you and presumably like you. So they are the most likely to be willing to buy your eBook.

Fourth, you need to market through other people. Arrange exchanges with everyone you can. The more people who are recommending your book to their customers the more likely that you will create a strong pent-up demand. If you have 1 person recommending you to their 1000 customers and getting you 10 sales -- that's not going to create a best seller. But getting 100 people doing the same thing will gain you

1000 sales... enough to get you on the bestseller list.

Fifth, think outside the box. Yes, it's nice to make money by having a best seller. But the point is to have a best seller. If you have to wait one book to make the profit it may still be worthwhile. So... can you figure out ways to buy copies of your eBook? Have a contest and give the top 100 people a copy of your eBook. Or buy a copy for every person in your customer list. Buy copes and mail them to your top fifty prospects.

Lightning Source UK Ltd.
Milton Keynes UK
UKHW010706110721
386955UK00001B/175